Jump your SaaS Sales Career

By Colby Stoker

2

Table of Contents

Preface……………...……………………..4

Before You Start……...………………..9

Prospecting……………...………………15

Outreach…………………...…………22

Customer Centricity……………...……..34

CRM……………………………...…….40

Pipeline Management…………………....42

Time Management…………….....…………47

Conclusion…………………………….51

Terms…………………………………...54

Preface

In the summer of 2016, I started working for AdRoll, an online advertising platform. Thanks to my brother-in-law Conner who also worked there, they somehow hired me even with no real sales experience and a less than outstanding interview. We had four weeks of "in class" training. We were taught about sales processes and policies, the tools that we would be using every day, and the ins and outs of the product that we would be selling. We talked about stages in our CRM tool Salesforce, leads, accounts, opportunities, AEs, SDRs, SaaS, technical implementation of our product, how to find new contact information and many other things that due to my lack of sales and tech experience all seemed like a foreign language to me. By the time the four weeks were over, I was overwhelmed and discouraged. There were about 20 others in my training cohort all of which seemed to be grasping everything quickly and were confident about all of the material that was covered. I definitely didn't feel that I was at the level that they were at or where I needed to be to start selling.

Fast forward a year and a half to the end of 2017. I was one of the top performing reps for the year and earned a trip to an all-inclusive resort with my wife. During the previous year and a half, I achieved over 255% of my revenue goal and 175% of my new business/clients goal. In the month of November, I set a record for the small business program at AdRoll with 23 closes in one month, our quota was six. I hit quota every single month and up to that point, and to my knowledge, still hold the record, for being the quickest rep to ramp and carry on a full quota. Fast forward another year to the end of 2018 and I am now a mid-market account executive and am currently pacing to hit 160% of our quarterly goal.

The reason I share this with you is that I am convinced anyone can succeed in sales. No matter what your previous experience, current knowledge, or personality is. If you are willing to put in the work, then it is possible. In Angela Duckworth's book "Grit" she talks about the importance of not putting others on a podium and thinking that they have achieved what they have because of natural abilities or God-given gifts. If we begin to put top sellers on a podium like this, that is when we begin to lose. Mentally this blocks us from being able to achieve those same things. Instead, if hard work, perseverance, and consistency are what we focus on then anyone can be great and succeed in sales.

This book is aimed to help those just starting out in sales to gain a good understanding of some of the fundamentals in SaaS sales. Compiled in this book are conversations that I have had many times with new reps to help them quickly grasp concepts and jumpstart their growth. Multiple corporate trainers who oversee the training and development of sales teams at different companies have been able to share with me where they constantly see knowledge or talent gaps with those beginning in SaaS sales. This book contains principles addressed at closing those gaps and what enabled me to quickly go from not knowing anything about sales to being a top performer. Not only have my experiences helped me write this book, but over 60 other sellers with a combined experience of over 250 years in SaaS sales from big corporations such as Google, Facebook, Adobe, Salesforce, and Oracle to smaller startups such as Shiplr and Impartner. These individuals are in positions from business development reps to enterprise account executives and to vice presidents of sales at companies. They have shared some of their tips and strategies for success pertaining to SaaS sales and all of their perspectives and experiences have helped shape and develop this book.

Many sellers have expressed their wish to better understand some of the jargon involved with sales before they started. If you are unfamiliar with some of the basic terms in sales it may be beneficial for you to skip to the last chapter which is defining some key terms, many of which are used throughout this book.

Something I realize is that entire books can be written about each of the different topics we cover in this book. There are many other books on specific topics that will be able to help up-level you further in specific topics such as negotiation, time management, overcoming objections or closing a deal as they are focused on those specific topics and go much more in depth. Basic fundamentals proved to work by not only me, but many other experienced sellers in various industries, and will be covered in this book to help those beginners grasp what it will take to see success.

Industry trends are different, objections and barriers differ in different products, sales cycles vary greatly, and many other things make specific techniques or practices difficult to translate between different jobs and positions. These principles discussed can be implemented by anyone in any industry be a better seller because of it.

In Malcolm Gladwell's book, "Outliers", he discusses that many seemingly successful individuals throughout history, and still today, have done so through a mixture of being put in good situations and then taking advantage of those situations and opportunities. In my relatively short career in SaaS sales, I have been able to achieve things I never thought was possible for me, this quickly, or this early on in my life. It has financially allowed me to do more than I ever expected at this age from traveling with my wife to being able to get an early start investing in real estate. The number of opportunities and doors that have been opened to me because of my experience and track record of performance has amazed me. While I am not trying to say that I am an outlier, I am trying to help you see that if you have an opportunity to get into tech sales and take advantage of it by educating yourself and putting in consistent hard work it will pay off. Tech sales is a great place to be and you will set yourself up for the future in a variety of ways if you do your part and take advantage of it.

Before You Start

There are a handful of tips that are helpful to know when starting out in sales that don't fall into a specific category of the job, but are still just as important to know and implement as other techniques and principles found in this book. These tips have to deal with how to create your own luck, the importance of following sales policy, helping others and achieving goals.

One of the first things that I quickly realized when starting out in sales, is that sales is a numbers game. The more people that you are able to get in front of -- the more chances you have to set an appointment -- and the more chances you have to close a deal. The saying that everyone has heard,

"Work smarter not harder," definitely has some truth to it; in order to maximize success and results you need to be strategic in the way you work, have processes set in place, and you need to be as efficient as possible. Unfortunately, at times that quote ends up being an excuse for some people, and they don't put in as much effort as they should be putting in. You will quickly find that there is a very strong correlation between effort and performance. In order to close deals, you need to be sending emails and be making dials on the phone. That is the only way that progress is going to happen. You get out what you put in. Sifat Ali, an Account Executive from Linkedin feels what separates top performers from others is, "A combination of working hard and working smart. Hours need to be put in doing highly efficient tasks. Mastery of this typically results in high performance." You really do need to have thought and strategy behind the effort. Doing things for the sake of doing them won't have the same impact as doing them with a specific purpose. You have probably heard people say that they create their own luck, that is how it works in sales. As you put in a lot of effort you will find yourself creating your own luck and putting yourself in a great position to succeed.

You will likely hear a lot about sales policy. Sales policy includes the rules, guidelines, and parameters that you are required to stay within. It may be a variety of different things such as what size of businesses you can reach out to, the region or territory of the business, and when you are allowed to reach out to specific businesses. Whatever role that you are in will have different policies that you are supposed to follow. FOLLOW THESE RULES!! There are a lot of things that you can do to violate these policies and cover them up, which I am not going to go into. Just DON'T DO IT. It will catch up with you, later on, I have seen a handful of reps do this and it hurts the culture of the team, the relationship with them and management, and likely future opportunities because they are slowly deteriorating their network. You may at some time come across a unique situation that is in a grey area. If you are unsure about it, then be transparent with your manager. When trying to decide whether you may need approval for something always err on the side of caution. I have had a few times where I have asked my manager about the situation and they have either given me approval or gotten approval from someone else for me to work an opportunity. Steven Porter, an AE from Workday said some important advice that he would give someone who is just starting out in sales is to, "Consider the impact of decisions on your future network. After 24 years, I have known people for a long time." I haven't been working near as long as Steven, but I already see the importance of networking and how that has helped me, don't jeopardize the trust with your relationships in your network. Don't sell your birthright for a mess of pottage.

Zig Ziglar says, "You can have everything you want in life if you help enough other people get what they want in life." There is a lot more to that quote than I currently understand, but I have already been able to see this principle working many times in my short career. As I have taken the time to help others, it ends up helping me out as well. Quickly after I started in sales, I volunteered to help mentor others just starting out. I would take some time to do mock calls with them, help them on cold calls, go through demos, and coach them through managing their pipelines. As I spent time helping them up-level themselves it forced me to up-level myself as well. I had to make sure I was giving them accurate information and feedback, meaning I had to hold myself to a higher standard than I would have if I wasn't actively helping others out. This is something I really believe accelerated my growth and helped to shorten the learning curve at the beginning. Find ways to help other individuals; this can be difficult to do when you are the one just beginning and are needing most of the help, but you will find opportunities to help others if you are looking for them. In the book, The Go Giver, by Bob Burg, it talks about how when you decide to do things for others it ends up benefiting you even more. Forget yourself for a bit and find ways to help others.

Goals… that is another topic that has countless amounts of books written on it, a lot of them have very valuable information, but yet they seem to contradict at times. I believe different strategies, philosophies and tactics can help different individuals. While I definitely believe that goals are crucial to push ourselves to reach our potential in every area of life we need to use them correctly. As James Clear says in his book Atomic Habits, "Winners and Losers have the same goals." Simply having a goal isn't enough to get the job done, no team starting a game wants to lose, both teams have a goal to win, yet one of them doesn't. Everyone wants to do well at a job, everyone starting out in sales wants to hit their quota. It comes down to ACTION! Setting a plan and actually executing that plan. Make things happen. Luckily everyone can be a winner in sales and achieve their goals if they work at it. As Jim Rohn said, "Discipline is the bridge between goals and accomplishment."

There are a handful of books I have read that have impacted the way I think about how to execute my plans to reach my goals, they are very different, and some of the ideas will click with different types of people. In Grant Cardone's book, The 10x Rule, he discusses his thoughts on goal setting and the action needed to reach goals. Grant Cardone has achieved a lot in his life by acquiring real estate, building a large company, and publishing books. He says he has been able to make these things happen by thinking about what he wants and then multiplying the results he wants by 10. He then thinks about what action needs to take place to reach that goal and multiplies that by 10. He teaches that to reach your goals you need to do 10 times more than you think you need to. Massive action is what he is teaching.

Other books such as the Slight Edge, Atomic Habits, and The Compound Effect take a more subtle approach that is easier to digest and feels a lot more attainable at times. While these books aren't primarily focussed on goals, they are focussed on how small actions can lead to huge changes and results. They discuss a variety of strategies that are very easy to do, but also very easy not to do. For example, it would be very easy to make the decision to eat a carrot instead of a cookie for a snack, but it would be very easy not to make that decision as well. Making that choice probably won't have that much of an impact on your health, but what if you made that decision every single day for years? The effects are massive and the tiny decision that seems insignificant at the moment adds up and compounds over time. The same can be said about our decisions every day on the job. It is not hard to make one more call each day or to send one more email out. It would be very easy to do those things, but would also be very easy not to. After a day or two, it probably is not going to have much of an impact on your results, if any at all. What if you just sent one more email and picked up the phone one more time each morning and each afternoon, and did that every single day for a year. That is hundreds of more opportunities for yourself to get the results you are wanting and can set you apart from everyone else.

Whether you are going to attack your goals with massive action or going to have a steady consistent mindset of doing just a bit more every day -- make sure that it happens. Don't leave your goals in the back of your head just to come up short. Make a plan and execute on that

Prospecting

Prospecting encompasses a variety of different things from finding different businesses or accounts that you want to reach out to, finding correct contact info, and getting in touch with the right person. Prospecting is one of the most important topics and concepts in sales. Whether you are an LDR, SDR/BDR, or an AE, prospecting is crucial. Prospecting is the lifeblood for your success. You need to be constantly finding new accounts to fill your pipeline with.

Consistent prospecting is one of the main things that sets average performers from top performers. It is extremely important, but often gets overlooked and put off. Many reps often will choose to do other things such as admin work over prospecting. While the consequences of this aren't shown immediately, they definitely do reveal themselves in a month or so. If you stop prospecting today, it likely won't affect you and your results for 1-2 months depending on the sales cycle of your product. Many times when someone's pipeline is stale or cold and they don't have very many accounts in their lower funnel it is because of the lack of prospecting that took place weeks or months prior to that.

In Jeb Blount's book, Fanatical Prospecting, which is a great book that goes much more in depth on this topic, he says that the best performers prospect when times are good, when times are bad, and when they don't want to. They are obsessed with prospecting. I have seen this countless amounts of time with reps. Many of them get lazy with working the top of their pipeline and working on getting in touch with new decision makers and then their pipelines end up getting stale and they wonder why. Often times they misdiagnose their problem and think that they aren't good at closing or driving urgency. In reality, it was because they got lazy with their prospecting at some point in the previous weeks and it is catching up to them now. If you ever get to this point it is often too late to do anything about it. If it is the end of the month or quarter and you are trying to find a couple last deals to move the needle for you, but your pipeline has gone cold because of the lack of prospecting you have done, it is too late. Prospecting at this point likely won't yield the results you are needing that soon. Yes, you need to start doing it immediately so that you can get back on track and get new deals moving to your mid and lower funnel, but it will take time. Make sure you are consistently prospecting so that you don't get caught in that position that so many reps find themselves in.

When it comes to finding new businesses that you are wanting to reach out to, there are so many different ways to go about it. Inbound leads, trade shows, past customers, your CRM, social media, referrals, and a variety of other ways. I am not going to take the time to go into each of these in detail. Depending on your industry and ideal customer, specific strategies will work better for you. No matter what industry you are in make sure that you have multiple strategies that you can go to. Only having one source to find new businesses to fill up your pipeline can hurt you. Utilizing multiple strategies will help you find more businesses, as well as help you mix things up a bit so that prospecting doesn't get too monotonous. It will also help you down the road if you switch the role you are in, or your job, you may find yourself needing to find completely different types of businesses. You may find that the way that you previously were prospecting won't work well, and if that is all you know, then you have to start from scratch. Mix it up, and find a few things that work well for you. Don't put all of your eggs in one basket.

One of the best ways to find new businesses is through referrals. This is something I have found is difficult to often remember, but it is so simple to actually do. Jeb Blount, the author of Fanatical Prospecting, says that he has read dozens of different books on referrals and they can all be summarized into a couple of points. Create an amazing customer experience and ask for a referral. There have been times where a company I have been working with has been extremely pleased and they tell someone else about me and what I am doing and that business reaches out to me! These are some of the best leads to get! Someone that they know and trust told them to have a discussion with me. I have seen success from getting referrals from others, but oftentimes don't even ask for referrals from the companies I am helping. Why is this? For me, it is because I am not even thinking about it. A good time to ask for a referral is when someone has recently started out using a product and is having a good experience, or is about to start using it and is excited. My mindset is usually focused on closing the deal or handing them over to an account manager, but a slight shift in mindset to be thinking of asking for referrals would easily pay off.

Once again, it is hard to share specific techniques for prospecting because the effectiveness of each method will likely vary greatly depending on the industry you are in. A couple of tools that I have found to be beneficial to use for prospecting, that can translate well to other industries, are free extensions on Google Chrome called Alexa Traffic Rank and another one called Similar Sites. When you are on a website and click on one of those extensions it will provide other suggestions of websites that are similar to the one you are currently on. The extension will take into consideration a handful of different factors when determining suggestions of similar websites such as if the site is e-commerce, a blog, B2B, retail, and the size of the website (based on estimated site traffic). You can pull up a website of your ideal customer and then start finding sites that are similar to it. I will open a handful at a time, close out of the ones that I am not interested in looking into further and keep the ones up that I would like to start working. The companies that look like an ideal target through the initial extension search, I can then repeat the process and continue to click on extensions that are similar to that one. This process can keep you busy for a very long time.

Something that has worked very well for me to keep me organized and help me be efficient with this method of prospecting is to create a folder on my bookmarks bar of the browser I am using and title it "Prospecting". At the end of my day or the end of my prospecting session, I will have a handful of sites opened that I want to continue to use for prospecting by using the extension to find other similar sites. I will put all of these I haven't gotten to yet in that prospecting folder on the bookmarks bar of my browser. The next day when I am prospecting I can quickly open those websites up and start prospecting from there; once I have exhausted all of the similar sites from a particular website I will remove it from the prospecting folder that is bookmarked. If you use this method for prospecting make sure you are doing your due diligence to make sure it is within sales policy and to check it in your teams CRM.

Use your CRM to your advantage. New startups might find this method more difficult because of the lack of history of reps reaching out to businesses, but the majority of times this is a great way to find some low hanging fruit. You can pull many different lists or reports in your CRM to sift through. While looking for accounts to start reaching out to in the CRM, try looking for ones that have had a conversation with someone at our company in the past, but for whatever reason, they said the timing wasn't right and to circle back around in the future. Many times I have reached out to these and the timing happened to be a lot better for them this time around and their buying window was coming up.

Also, when using the CRM to look at accounts that have been reached out to in the past you will usually find a lot of businesses who have told your company that they aren't interested. If these conversations happened close to a year ago or longer I may be interested in taking another stab at it. There are a few reasons for this: they may have more of a need for your product now based on different challenges they are facing, updates or changes to the product you are selling may be able to help you position it better to them and their needs, and people change jobs more frequently than ever now and there is a good chance that the decision maker is someone new and worth reaching out to. However, be wise while doing this, if 9 months ago the decision maker said they weren't interested because they are in a two-year contract with someone already, just because it is a new decision maker doesn't mean it is worth reaching out to; most likely they are still in that contract so don't waste your time.

Very often will I come across accounts that I would like to reach out to, but for a variety of different reasons such as other contracts, seasonality, product launches, or other internal challenges they aren't ready to have a conversation with me. To help stay organized I will copy the URL or link of the account in my CRM and create a calendar event for the morning of the date when I feel would be a good time to reach back out. For example, if it is January 5th and I come across an account that has been reached out to by our company recently and the DM said that they are completely rebranding and launching a new website in April and they don't want to do any advertising in the meantime, then I will create a calendar event for the end of March to reach out to that account to start up the conversation again when the timing is most likely better for them. When that day at the end of March comes that I set the calendar event for I will see the calendar event and start reaching out to it, hopefully near their buying window. If I didn't do this, I would forget about the account that I saw or would have to do a lot of digging and sifting to find it again, which takes a lot of time. You can use this technique in a variety of different ways, it doesn't just have to be for accounts you find while going through your CRM.

Depending on your product, contacting businesses that have used your product in the past, also known as orphans, can sometimes be a useful thing to fill part of your pipeline. These can many times be low hanging fruit. Many times I have reached out to these accounts and they have told me they are ready to get things going with us again. I have had a handful of very quick and easy closes with these orphan companies. They aren't always an easy close, so I wouldn't recommend exclusively reaching out to these, but having a handful of them in your pipeline at all times can be helpful. You will need to check on your own sales policy when it comes to these. It may be the responsibility of someone in a different role to contact these accounts. For my team, there is a specified amount of time after someone has churned or stopped using our product that we have to wait before we can reach out to them. I oftentimes will make calendar events for these orphan companies when I come across them. That way I am ready to reach out to them when that time period has passed. Whatever your team's policy is, make sure you are following it.

Outreach

As soon as I find an account that I want to start working I immediately reach out to them so that I don't let it fall through the cracks and forget about it. Before you can reach out, you need to find the best contact information. One of the most important things to remember when outreaching is making sure that you are reaching out to the right person. You should know who the typical decision maker is that you are trying to get in touch with, whether it is a c-level executive, a controller, marketing manager, VP of sales, director of IT, or so on. Being able to figure out who that person is and how to contact them can take some time, but is required for success.

There are a variety of different ways and tools to use to find the decision maker within the company. Since there are so many tools to help with finding the decision maker, I am only going to talk about a couple of tools that are free for everyone to use. LinkedIn is probably the most common way to find out who the decision maker is; you can also pay for other tools within LinkedIn, but it is free to just search a person or company and find some information on them. Sometimes on a LinkedIn profile, it will have contact information to reach that person at, I have found that this is more rare than common, but it definitely does happen. Once I have the name of the person, that I found on LinkedIn, I will go to mailtester.com which is a free service that validates whether an email address is legitimate or not. Here I try a handful of combinations to see if any of them are valid. For example, if I found on LinkedIn the person that I want to get in touch with is Chris Adams that works at abc.com I will go to Mail Tester and try the following different combinations Chris@abc.com, Chrisadams@abc.com, Chris.adams@abc.com, adams.chris@abc.com, cadams@abc.com, c.adams@abc.com, chris.a@abc.com, or chrisa@abc.com. Usually one of these will work. When mail tester checks an email address it will either be highlighted as red, meaning not a valid email address, or green, for a valid email address. You can find the majority of your email addresses this way.

Occasionally you won't be able to find the correct email address for the person or even the name of the person. When you run into this situation you have a variety of other options. You can try to broadly contact the department you are looking to get in touch with by testing email addresses such as IT@abc.com, marketing@abc.com, finance@abc.com and then try to get in touch with the right person that way. Jimmy Woodward, a BDR at Salesforce, says that he will call the wrong person on purpose. He can then get more information on the person, like a name, email address, or extension, but also use it as a referral by saying "Bob sent me your way..". Other people can be a great way to find contact information. A lot of times people are happy to help, although, often you will find gatekeepers or influencers who don't want to give out information on the decision maker. They will usually try to brush me off on the phone by saying just fill out a form on the website or email info@abc.com. If this is the case I will say, "Great, and who should I address my email/inquiry to?" At this point in the call, the gatekeeper already knows the title of the person I am trying to get in touch with, as that is one of the first things I said on the call. Many times they will say the name of the person you can address it to like, Chris Adams. Boom. That is all you need to then find the best email address for Chris using Mail Tester.

An AE from a top vendor said, "While prospecting I got an out of office reply which listed the email of a senior stakeholder so I reached out to her instead. It turned out they were weeks from renewing with their current vendor, we had a couple of meetings and signed a $1.6 million 3 year contract with them. The lesson was, always collect details from out of office emails." There are plenty of ways to find contact information so be creative, like this story illustrates, and find different methods and tools to help you. Start off by talking to others in your role who are seeing good success.

Once I get the best contact information, I start reaching out to them. Many people will immediately call them to start off. Typically, I will immediately put them in a sequence using Outreach.io. One of my favorite tools to use is Outreach.io when reaching out to businesses. You can set up a sequence of emails and calls at a specific cadence that you would like. For example, I will want my first email to go out immediately then if no one replies I will wait to call in a couple of days, then send an email a day later, etc. Outreach makes this happen automatically. The emails will be sent out when you have scheduled them to and each morning it will inform you which accounts you need to call that day. Regardless of whether you use Outreach or another tool like it I would strongly recommend that you have your own sequence and cadence set up that you manually go through with each account. The more processes you have in place the more efficiently you can work. So make sure you take control over putting these processes and systems in place for your outreach.

Before I used Outreach.io I had to manually send all of the emails and pull up the account in the CRM to call them. There are a variety of ways that you can keep organized with this. The way that worked best for me was to create templates in Gmail that I regularly sent out and I would name them based on what order I would send them out in. For example, the first email I sent out was named "1", the email that got sent after that one was named "2", and so on. Obviously, there were other templates for unique or different situations, but for the majority of the time, if I hadn't reached the decision maker yet, that was the order I would send emails. Always remember to call the decision maker in between each email, as well.

Somewhere in your sequences/cadences make sure that you are attempting to reach them in more ways than just cold calling and emailing. Social

25

media is a great way to reach decision makers; you can oftentimes bypass the gatekeeper through this method. Send them a connection, note on LinkedIn or try to interact with one of their recent posts. These will help your cold outreaching be a bit warmer. Every salesperson calls and emails so try to be a bit different and be creative to stand out from the others.

When sending emails make sure that you are personalizing them. Chances are if you are wanting to get in touch with a person there are other reps at different companies wanting to as well. So make sure that you stand out by doing some research and putting some thought into your emails for better response rates. When looking for things to include in the emails make sure that you check LinkedIn and their business website. Include things in the email that are relevant to that person and the industry they are in. Make sure you keep your emails and subject lines short, the longer they are the less chance you have to hear back from them. Typically, four sentences are enough to show them you did some research, call out a business you have helped in the past, and add a call to action such as scheduling an appointment. Many people open their emails on their phones, which makes brevity even more crucial. Less is more.

Make the email about the prospect and not about yourself. If your email is all about you; why YOU want to talk with them and why YOU are reaching out to them, then you won't hear back from them as often as you would if you were focussed on them. Focus on what their position is, what they are interested in, and what they will get out of scheduling an appointment with you. When using tools such as Outreach or Yesware you can look at the different

26

open and reply rates of your different emails and subject lines to optimize your emails that are going out. Keep experimenting with new emails or tweaking existing ones to see what effect it has on your open and reply rates.

You need to have a balance when it comes to personalizing the emails. You need a healthy mix of quantity and quality. Sometimes I lack the quality because I am focussing on the quantity and that ends up hurting me. The opposite can also be true though. Many times I have seen reps who are so concerned about doing so much research and personalization that it takes them so much time before they ever get an email out or ever make a phone call. This really limits their potential. Find a balance between the two that works for you. Spend some time with someone who is performing well in your industry or at your company to figure out how many people you need to get in touch with. If they are reaching out to 30 accounts a day, you may need to reach out to even more than 30 prospects due to your lack of experience. Then figure out how much time you can allocate reaching out to each one, based on the amount of time you are allocating towards getting in touch with decision makers.

Also, do not give up. If you are sending high-quality emails that are worth it for a prospect to read, then give them a chance to respond to you, don't give up too early. Trent Dressel a BDR at Qualtrics said, "Our cadence has 16 steps consisting of emails and calls, as you could imagine the deeper in the cadence the prospect gets, the contact rate goes down. I set a meeting on a step 14 contact who said the only reason he would take my call is because of

27

the persistence of challenging and leaving VM's. Never stop calling until they tell you otherwise."

Cold calling is probably one of the most difficult and hated parts of the job, but is also one of the most important. Many people will say that cold calling doesn't work anymore and it is a waste of time. I do agree that it has changed, but I disagree that it doesn't work at all anymore. There definitely is a place for picking up the phone and making dials. As a seller, you have to be a bit more prepared now than in the past, people are more used to getting cold calls from sellers, so they are programmed to get off the phone as quickly as possible. Make sure you know who you are calling and be prepared to speak to the decision maker; you likely will only have that initial opportunity to make a good enough impression to further the conversation. There have been times when I have been making dials and not having much luck getting through the gatekeepers. One day while I was cold calling I was receiving a constant stream of gatekeepers and voicemails; when finally -- the decision maker ends up answering one of my calls. I was preparing myself to leave another voicemail or talk to another gatekeeper so when I finally got to a person I had actually been wanting to talk to, I was caught off guard and was all over the place. This made it seem like I lacked confidence in the product and to the person on the other end of the phone, I was not worth their time. Be prepared, so that you are not caught off guard and don't miss your opportunity. It's better to be expecting the DM and be caught off guard for the voicemail than it is to be expecting a voicemail and get caught off guard when the DM gets on the phone. Speaking to the DM has a substantially higher success rate of moving the needle than leaving a voicemail or talking to a gatekeeper.

When you first get the decision maker on the phone make sure you tell them who you are and why you are calling; once again, just like the emails, make sure it is about them and not you. Be focused on them and why you calling them out of the blue is good for them. After that, ask for what you are looking for, which is usually to set an appointment, and tell them what they will get out of the appointment and why they would want to do that. For example, a script may go something like…. "Hi Chris, this is Colby from xyz. Since you are the director of X, due to the season, I am sure that you are really bogged down with Y. We have helped the director at [Insert similar company in the industry] with this by doing A, B, and C. Do you have 25 minutes on Thursday at 1 or 3 to discuss your business to see if this will help you as well?"

There are thousands of variations to this script and many may be better than this, but the point is to keep it short and to the point. Make sure you are letting them know what is in it for them. Why would they take the appointment with you? If you say "I would like to set an appointment to talk about our great product." You likely are not going to see much success. They are busy, they don't care what you want and what you like; but, if you show them what they need and how it will help them your results will skyrocket.

Like mentioned above, there will be plenty of times when you are only able to contact to reach a gatekeeper or a voicemail. Take advantage of those as well. If I am unable to get past the gatekeeper, I try to get as much information out of them as I can about the DM. The first thing I try to figure out is their name which will allow me to find an email address, trying to gather other information such as a phone number, extension number, times of the day they are in, etc. can also be very beneficial for your future outreaching. Make sure that you are nice to the gatekeepers and treat them with respect. This is something that shouldn't need to be talked about much, because you should treat everyone you come across with respect. It can be frustrating talking to a gatekeeper that won't give you much information or is extremely short with you, but the more polite you are the higher chance you have at getting something out of it.

When getting to the voicemail of a decision maker make sure you use that time productively for your sake and for the decision makers sake. Just like on a cold call make sure you are quick and to the point. Tell them who you are, why you are calling, what's in it for them, and how they can reach you via the phone or email. Callbacks from voicemails don't happen frequently, but they definitely do. There have been multiple occasions I have had someone return my call after I left a voicemail. Don't leave one every time you call and don't leave the exact same voicemail every time either. Typically I will leave around 3 voicemails with the same person. Just like at other times when on the phone, be yourself and be real. Don't sound like a stereotypical salesman with a wannabe glamourous voice.

Cold calling can be very monotonous at times when you aren't seeing results and are facing a lot of rejection, but persistence pays off. Tanner Rappleye, an AE at Shiplr shared a story about when he was a

BDR at a previous company. He said, "I was trying to get in touch with a CFO of a fortune 500 company that I had called and called to set a meeting for my Account Executive. I probably called him 50+ times in 2 weeks. I finally got a hold of him and set a meeting. Then when the meeting happened he told my Account Executive "Oh man I love Tanner and his persistence." That one line showed me that my hard work to get him on the phone was worth it, and didn't make him mad, and it really takes hard work to get the success that's needed." Tanner also said, "Just call. Don't hesitate to call someone 3+ times a day. You want to get a hold of someone specific... call them until you get them on the phone or move on to someone else." It really is a numbers game. Whether it is getting in front of enough accounts or getting in front of a specific account enough times.

You can find countless articles and resources about when the best time to make cold calls are. You can dive into those yourself and see which makes the most sense for you because many of them say different things and contradict each other. Success on cold calls can come at any time of the day on any day throughout the week, not only have I seen it myself, but I have seen it with other reps as well. Except for one time. There is a time when success will not come through cold calling, and that is when you are not cold calling. It sounds obvious, but it is the truth. If you are sitting there making excuses about why you shouldn't be cold calling you will not see results and get anything out of it; believe me, I have been there, but if you do put in the effort and put off your lazy tendencies you will see results and you will move the needle on accounts.

31

Jerry Parnell an AE at Workday gives some good advice when it comes to this. Jerry says, "Make sure you understand the level of cold calling and prospecting that is required in the specific sales job. Rejection is not easy and a majority of sales job require high amounts of cold calling so make sure you spend quality time in the interview discussing this important part of the job." In Fanatical Prospecting, Jeb Blount says that the typical sales rep gets more rejection before nine in the morning than the average person gets in a year. There are days where this is definitely true! Cold calling and rejection go hand in hand and they are a part of every sales job. Make sure you understand that and mentally prepare for it. You need to let the rejection run off like water on a duck's back.

For the majority of sellers, cold calling is one of their least favorite parts of the job. In Brian Tracy's book, Eat That Frog he talks about procrastination and how to get over it. The premise of the book is that if you eat a frog in the morning, you won't have to do anything more difficult for the rest of the day. This principle is the same when applied to cold calling, if you get it done in the morning, then the rest of the day seems a lot easier. If you put off all of your cold calling until the afternoon, you may not have enough left in the tank to put in the necessary effort you need to get it done. There have been many times that someone on my team, or myself, has, for whatever reason, postponed calls until the afternoon and almost every time the quantity and quality of the calls are lower than when we complete them in the morning. There may be specific people that you are waiting to call until the afternoon for specific reasons such as that is when they are in the office, time zone difference, etc, but the majority of the time the morning works great. So unless you are superhuman, just eat the frog and get it done in the morning.

Customer Centricity

Once you start reaching out, you will begin to get replies to your emails, and will hear back from your decision makers. You will also begin to set up appointments. In all of these various types of communications that you have with the potential customer, you need to remain customer-centric at all times. It is human nature to think about ourselves and our situations; because of this, we come short many times to effectively communicate things to others and add value to them and their situations.

Many of the sellers that answered questions for me at some point brought up the importance of putting the customer first and doing what is right for them. Here are a few examples.

Eric Young at Linkedin said, "No matter the product or service, your solution is in support of a loftier priority. Focusing on helping more people and companies leads to success in sales."

In a blog post titled, Stop Throwing Spaghetti, Alex Luxenberg, an AE at Facebook, says, "The first step in effectively building a pitch is understanding your client and what motivates them (personally and professionally). You are better off selling your client one product, that is going to work really well for them, than selling them a few that don't solve their challenges or aren't built for them to achieve their goals."

Dan Mayer a regional VP of sales at Salesforce said, "When I first started out in Sales I thought that learning the product I sold was the most important thing I could do for the customer. When I look back now, I sold a lot on product features/bells and whistles. My advice to those starting in Sales is to understand the external factors facing an industry. It's all about the customer. Understand the undeniable shift taking place. Help the customer know there will be winners and losers for those who do not make a change in their industry. Help your customer understand the value drivers your solution will have on saving money or making money if they made the switch to your solution."

Sales really is about providing solutions to problems that others have. As a seller, you are trying to figure out what they are currently experiencing and how you can offer something that will help them and solve different challenges and problems that they are facing. How do we expect to do that if we don't put them and their needs first? Yet, time and time again sellers try to push their own agenda and are not seeing things from the perspective of the customer.

Julian Mackrel at Chorus takes things a step further, he says to put in the work to make a prospect successful (even if their not buying your product just yet) will build credibility as a true resource. They'll come back to you repeatedly because they trust you. That advice is great, but can be difficult for sellers to follow at times. Sometimes helping the prospect out doesn't mean selling them your product. If you are doing your due diligence while prospecting and reaching out to your ideal customers then the majority of the time there may be an opportunity for that business and you to work together, however as Julian and others have seen there are occasions when it doesn't make sense at the time. The best thing that you can do then is to be the expert; educate the prospect on what you feel would be the most beneficial for them at that time, and reconnect later down the road with them.

You will see many different questions, concerns, and objections. Always put the customer first. Often times, we are trained on how to handle certain objections and many times these aren't customer-centric, they may resolve an issue momentarily, but it isn't building value in the long run. When Jason Thomas an AE at Salesforce comes across objections he tries to understand the reason for the objection. He typically reframes them in his mind as 'concerns' and puts himself in their shoes, trying to see the risk that they're attempting to mitigate. If we all thought a bit more like that it would do us well. We are so quick to forget about what is important in the customer's eyes and the risk they feel when bringing on new products.

Scott Padgett, a senior sales executive at Amazon Web Services (AWS), says to understand the customer's challenge and work backwards. Too often, inexperienced sales reps do not listen to their customers. They want to immediately jump in and sell their widget or service. Immature sales reps view everything as a nail and their product as the hammer. By truly listening to a customer's challenge(s) and working backwards from their problem, you can really solve it and build trust. Do this and the sales will come naturally." Jerry Parnell also echoes this same advice he puts it all in a doc and shares that doc with the customer. It has laid out all of the dates and who needs to be involved in each step. After he has this put together he asks the customer for their feedback to really make sure it is what the customer wants. Scott and Jerry are helping us understand that we are on the same team as the customer, we need to be working together with them towards a common goal. If each party has different goals, and they are not aligned, then the sale will not go smoothly and likely won't happen at all.

Recently AdRoll did a marketing campaign that consisted of videos from the companies customers. The customers explained what their experience was when beginning to use the AdRoll platform and thereafter. In one of the videos, the customer explained how he was new to his company and was extremely nervous when beginning to run advertising campaigns through AdRoll. He said he was actually sweating when the campaigns were turned on and he spent a lot of time just sitting and waiting for results to come in, scared that they wouldn't perform. They ended up performing great and that company is still using the platform. However, the point is that we don't realize how important these decisions are to these individuals that we are talking to. They may be new in a role or company and they are wanting to set a good beginning impression and they are nervous that if things don't go as expected when using the product you are discussing with them, then it will have negative effects on how upper management views them. There are numerous reasons and examples as to why someone is asking specific questions and why they may be hesitant to pull the trigger. Make sure that you are not trying to quickly push the sale through before they are more comfortable.

Don't get me wrong driving urgency is one of the most important things to moving a deal along and it is something that needs to happen, but you can't compromise being customer-centric. When it comes to driving urgency it is best done when, you've got it, you are putting the customer first. Another AE shared, "Work to a mutual plan with the customer that includes working back from a deadline. I.e. project kickoff they have to be ready for our end of quarter deadline. For example, go live 1st December, 25th November "provisioning software", 20th November Purchase order received, 19th November contract signed." Figure out what their needs are and when THEY need it. Then work backward with everything that needs to be done before that with specific deadlines.

Another great way to drive urgency, is to illustrate what the impact is if they do not implement your product. Let them know what the consequences are if they don't implement it. Many times you can figure out what they are missing out on each day that they decide to postpone implementing your product. Quantifying the impact of them implementing or not implementing your solution can help drive urgency. When illustrating the product's impact, include figures such as ROI, employee time, expenses, etc. All of this is focused around solving their problems, so when you illustrate the impact it is important to maintain that customer focused approach. Make sure you are coming up with solutions and using numbers that are relevant to them, if they are more worried about saving time than expenses make sure you are focussed on the impact it will have on their time rather than expenses.

Julian, who was mentioned earlier, sums up driving urgency by saying, "Identify the impact of the project, and present ROI. Identify emotional impact as well (how would this be good for my prospect's career, or for their team's performance). Every buyer has a personal need as well, and if you build a relationship to understand how to serve the company and that individual, success rates increase."

CRM

As a seller, you will spend a large chunk of your time in the CRM. Whether it is Salesforce, Hubspot, or another CRM, you will be using it a lot. The CRM holds a lot of information on all of the accounts that have been reached out to in the past, accounts that are currently being reached out to, current customers. You will also find many details on all of these contacts. The CRM can and should be one of your best friends. At times, it can be very tedious to update information in the CRM, but if you aren't keeping up on it, then it is going to hurt you.

There have been times after finishing an appointment I don't log very detailed notes, because I am trying to hurry, then, later on, I pull up the notes I logged from the appointment and there are details that aren't recorded and I can't remember. The only way to get that information again (unless your call was recorded), is to ask again. If they have already told you once it may hurt the relationship to have to ask them again. It likely won't make or break a deal, but in sales, you want to create your own luck as much as possible, and having to ask a potential customer the same questions twice isn't going to help.

Having the CRM up to date also helps management aid you. They have a handful of different reports and things they are looking at to see how you are performing, where your deals are at, and where you can improve. If the CRM lacks a lot of information and isn't updated it makes their job a lot more difficult when trying to help you get better. Likely, they will end up asking you questions that they aren't able to obtain from the CRM because it isn't there and that is going to take your time anyway. Being efficient with your time is one of the most important parts of the job, and the best way to be efficient with the CRM is to do it right the first time and keep it up to date and detailed.

Spend time to explore and become more familiar with your CRM. Many times a team or organization will find a few ways of looking at things in the CRM and always revert to those same tactics. There are likely many more ways you can find to manipulate and navigate the CRM that are more effective than the way everyone else is doing it. Don't just follow the same things everyone else is doing, use things that are working well for other top performers, but find other effective ways as well that others haven't found.

Pipeline Management

Pipeline management is another one of the things that separate top performers from everyone else. Knowing what deals you have coming through the pipeline, what the next steps are for each of these deals, what possible challenges you may face with each contact in your pipeline, how healthy your mid and upper funnels are currently, are all important things to know when managing your pipeline. Being able to stay organized and on top of these details allows you to more effectively work accounts and see more results.

Oftentimes a rep will only focus on one area and neglect the others which cause part of their pipeline to go stale. For example, a rep may spend a lot of time working on deals that are near closing and spend the rest of their time working on replacing those deals after they close with deals that they have recently started conversations with. If they spend all of their time on those two areas and don't put in the necessary effort to prospect and fill their pipeline up with other potential opportunities down the road then soon enough they will find that they don't have anything in their mid or lower funnel. Each area of your funnel and pipeline deserves and needs time and attention.

The CRM is what will help you keep your pipeline organized. Regularly look at how many accounts you are reaching out to and how many of them are in different stages of the sales cycle. Make sure that you are regularly reaching out to them as well. If you forget to or stop reaching out to an account for too long it strongly diminishes your chances of moving them down the funnel.

There are many different ways to stay on top of your pipeline. One that I have found most effective is by having different reports within the CRM that I look at each day. Each report is for different stages of my funnel. This way I can isolate the accounts that are near their close date and see what I need to do to continue to move them along, which accounts I am in conversation with the decision maker, and which accounts I have yet to get in touch with yet.

For my lower funnel, I make sure that I look at them each day to see what needs to be done that day to meet any deadlines. Usually, not too many things have to be done on the mid-funnel. Sometimes you will have to send them some content, or make sure an appointment is scheduled with them, but for the most part, it is usually waiting until your scheduled appointment with them before more needs to be done. On most days, the majority of my time is spent on my upper funnel. Reaching out to accounts to get in touch with a decision maker to set an appointment. When looking at my upper funnel I will organize it by looking at how long it has been since I last reached out. Usually, I want all of the accounts in my upper funnel to be touched at least every four days. Each day I will look at the accounts that are above four days since my last touch, and I will either call them, send the next email in a sequence to them, or decide to move on and stop reaching out to them.

Frank Matera at Qualtrics said, "I look at my pipeline daily to make sure I'm working on my top opportunities for the day. Have an expected close date and try to do everything to close by that date." You need to make sure that you are owning your deals and doing everything in your control to get them to close.

When it comes to organizing and prioritizing your pipeline, Pierce Buxton an enterprise AE at Amazon Web Services, says that the correct order to prioritize is: "1. Closing 2. Prospecting 3. Moving the chains. Most reps do it 1,3,2, but you always need to be filling the pipeline. Although you still want to give them a little attention, the deals in play will move themselves."

This is something that many times reps don't understand. You need to consistently be working on your upper funnel and prospecting. Obviously, those near closing are the priority, but it also can't be stressed enough how crucial the top of the funnel is as well.

Jerry Parnell who was mentioned earlier said that your pipeline is the main focus of your job and you need to make sure you set time aside to work on it. He also recommends looking at some of the top performers to see how they are staying on top of their pipeline and "borrow" their strategies.

Even when you are staying on top of your pipeline and getting in front of all of your accounts regularly you will still have some that end up going dark, meaning you haven't been able to get in touch with them. They have responded to you in the past, but for whatever reason, they aren't getting back with you anymore. You try to call them at different times of the day, you have sent multiple emails, and tried to reach them on Linkedin without any luck. As one of my past managers, Tess Bell would say, you are "friend zoned" and it is worse to be in the friend zone than to know that they just aren't interested because you can waste a lot of your time still going after them.

How do you know when to move on and when to keep trying to get in touch with a stale account? There is not one definitive answer for all situations, but you need to be smart about it. A couple of factors that should go into determining how much time you spend on it are the potential value or size of the account and the amount of interest that they previously expressed.

If you got in touch with the decision maker a while ago, but they did not sound very interested at all, then they ended up going stale, don't spend much time on it, likely they aren't interested. Rather, if you did speak with the decision maker and there seemed to be a lot of interest then it may be worth continuing to go after. One of the best things you can do is to stay in front of them regularly, by leaving voicemails and sending some relevant content over to them. The content you send can be in a variety of different ways such as updates to the product, case studies, blogs or articles, changes in the industry, or anything else that you feel is relevant.

One of my biggest deals that I closed came from an account that went dark for a while. They told me that they wanted to try the AdRoll platform out, but then stopped responding to my emails and calls. This went on for a few months. Two to three times a month I would send over different articles and case studies to them and leave a voicemail or two. Eventually, they responded to one of my emails and I ended up closing one of the largest deals I ever have.

Kaden Pope from Qualtrics shares a similar experience, he lost a deal that he worked countless hours on in June. Kaden said he was devastated when they decided to go another direction. He was relentless and kept touching base throughout their implementation process with their client. By October, they had reached out, admitted they had made a mistake and signed a contract worth twice than what it was in June. Don't give up on a deal.

If you feel there is interest on their side and there is good potential with the account, then be willing to be persistent, but don't get caught in this trap with small accounts that never seemed to be interested.

Time Management

Make sure that you are keeping your pipeline organized and reaching out regularly, getting accounts ready to close, leaving meticulous notes and details in the CRM, sending content to stale accounts, attending meetings, completing your demos and appointments, reading up on the industry, doing research on your potential customers, making cold calls, reaching out on Linkedin, finding more accounts to start reaching out to, and finding the best contact information. Oh, and make sure that you accomplish all of that in your eight hour day.

Time management is one of the most important parts of the job. You need to be efficient with your time. There are many important moving pieces in a sales position and you can't neglect any of them. One of the best ways to organize your time is to block time out throughout your day for specific things. Put time on your calendar every day that is dedicated to cold calling, going through your pipeline, finding new accounts, etc. If you block out adequate time for each activity, and don't let other things come in the way, then you will be able to get the job done.

In Gary Keller and Jay Papasan's book, The One Thing. It discusses how we are not able to multi-task so trying to do multiple things at once decreases the effectiveness of the activities and slows us down. They stress the importance of focusing on one thing, the thing that is most important at that moment, and not letting anything else get in the way of that.

One of the hardest things when it comes to managing your time, is limiting distractions. There are a variety of things that can make us lose focus from the task at hand such as phones, social media, conversations with co-workers, and the list goes on. Do your best to limit these as much as possible. You can turn your phone off or silent it, block social media from your computer, and isolate yourself at times from your co-workers. For me, one of the biggest challenges was hearing conversations my co-workers were having, specifically about the latest sports drama, and want to hop in. To help me avoid this, I started listening to podcasts or music while I worked, not to focus on what I was listening to, but to drown out the conversations around me.

Meetings can also get in the way of your working time. Some meetings are mandatory and there is no way around them, but there are some that are optional and may be best to skip from time to time to get more done. Often times I would choose not to go out to lunch with my team or to a movie they were going to for a team activity during the day if I felt that I was behind. Make sure that your work and hitting your quota is your priority and other distractions don't get in the way.

This year, there was a meeting scheduled with our team to go through our pipeline with our manager and update them on what we have that near to closing and the details around these accounts. This meeting took quite a while. It was a decent chunk of our Monday afternoons. The meeting was important though, it helped our manager better understand what we had coming up, so they could communicate this to upper management and better help us with these deals. I ended up suggesting that instead of having this meeting together as a team it be treated more like a one-on-one meeting so that not everyone had to be in the meeting at once listening to everyone else talk with the manager about their deals. My manager made the change and it freed up a lot of time on all of our calendars. You may be able to find similar ways that you can create time for yourself.

Also, make sure you are working the full eight hours every single day. During the beginning of my time in sales, one of the things that helped me ramp faster than everyone and quickly become a top performer was that I actually worked eight hours a day. Many people maybe got seven good hours of work in a day after you take out the time they spent on their phones, social media, walking around talking to others, etc. Getting a full extra hour of work a day in will quickly separate you from others, it may not seem like much at first, but it adds up. One extra hour a day from Monday through Friday would end up being 260 hours in a year which is 32 eight-hour working days or 37 seven-hour working days for everyone else. You are able to get so much done in that time. Efficiently working the entire time you are at work will set you apart.

One thing, that is important to note, is that well-timed breaks are important. There are a lot of benefits for disengaging for a short amount of time. I am not suggesting to completely eliminate all breaks of any kind. Well-timed breaks are important and I consider these SHORT breaks part of an efficient work day, but if you take too many, for too long, too frequently, you will run into problems. For more information about the importance of disengaging and when disengaging is most powerful, go read The Power of Full Engagement by Tony Schwartz and James Loehr.

Conclusion

There are a lot of different balls to juggle in a sales job and at times it can seem stressful, overwhelming, and even discouraging. If you do your best to have the right mindset and continue to improve every day it can be a very rewarding and exciting career. It can also be difficult to know where to start, but really, it is about jumping in and learning as you go. Alexa Moore said that there isn't anything she wishes she would have known before she started in sales because, "Failure is key, you need to fail in order to learn and get better." She also mentioned that people who aren't failing often aren't growing and learning as quick as the others. This is definitely true. If you wait until you are a master at sales and know the product inside and out before you start selling, then you will never get started.

Ben Seipal, an AE at Google, says, "Really dive into your pipe from the get-go. You know more than you think and will pick up what you need along the way. Don't worry about not knowing everything about your product. If you have the basics down solid, the rest comes with time." Taha Jafri also echoes this, "Nothing beats picking up the phone and putting in effort. Don't overthink things. Just have a conversation, be honest, and try to do what is in the best interest of the client."

Don't let paralysis by analysis stop you from getting started. Failure is part of the job, and the sooner you are able to get more comfortable with it, and accept it, the quicker you can start learning and fine-tuning your craft.

Dan Mayer said, "I've always learned more from my failures than my success stories. When you win a deal you get a lot of pats on the back. However, mistakes can be hidden because you won the deal." Turn your failures into victories by learning from them.

In Stephen R Covey's book the 7 Habits to Highly Effective People, he talks about the importance of sharpening the saw. Make sure you are spending adequate time sharpening yourself, by learning from your failures, as well as taking the time to read other books and listen to podcasts. Sales is something that no one can ever fully master, so no matter where you are in your career, there is always more to learn and techniques to perfect.

Make sure that you are constantly evaluating yourself in all of the different areas that were discussed. You should be looking at your processes and see where you can improve things. Rate yourself between 1-10 in the different categories and and every day try to get closer to a 10. There are always things you can be adding or taking away from your day-to-day processes that will allow you to be better.

In sales, there are some things you don't have control over, but there are many more things that you do have control over. Worry about the things you can control. You are the CEO of your life and your career, take ownership of it and make big things happen!

Terms

Many sellers said they wish they would have known the jargon and lingo that people use in sales and in their industry sooner in their career. Below is a list of a few basic terms you may come across that you aren't used to hearing. There are countless other terms unique to the industry you are in which aren't included here. Each industry is different so make sure you take time learning to speak like others in the industry. Robert Kiyosaki, an author and successful businessman, has said that you can tell how much someone knows based on the vocabulary that someone uses. Make sure that your vocabulary shows that you are someone with knowledge in your industry.

LDR- Lead development representative. Typically responsible for finding new leads and vetting them for others to reach out to.

ADM- Account development representative. Typically responsible for setting appointments for an AE by reaching out to inbound leads.

SDR- Sales development representative. Typically responsible for setting appointments for an AE. Some organizations have them working inbound leads, some just outbound calls/emails, and others both.

BDR- Business development representative. Setting outbound appointments for an AE.

AE- Account Executive. The closer. Usually will receive appointments from others, but many times works on setting their own appointments through outbound efforts as well.

DM- Decision maker. The person you are trying to reach in an organization that has the power to make the decision on moving forward with purchasing your product or not.

Gatekeeper- A person you have to go through before you can get to the decision maker, typically a secretary or someone who is answering calls for them.

Influencer- Someone who is involved in the decision-making process, but doesn't have the power to make the decision on their own.

ICP - Ideal customer profile. What your ideal customer looks like, based on different factors such as region, revenue, company size, etc.

CRM- Customer relationship management. Popular CRMs for sales teams are Salesforce and Hubspot.

They allow you to stay organized by keeping track of all of the accounts that you and the team are currently working and have worked in the past, with notes and details about each one.

Pipeline- Consists of all of the accounts that you are reaching out to anywhere in the sales process. Account- Usually referring to a company or business.

Upper Funnel- Typically referring to accounts that you haven't gotten in touch with the decision maker yet.

Mid Funnel- Usually referring to accounts that you have reached a decision maker, but aren't too far along in the sales process/cycle yet.

Lower Funnel- Accounts that are getting close to closing.

SaaS- Software as a service

ARPA/ASPA- Average revenue per account / average spend per account.

QBR- Quarterly business review, held by many businesses every quarter to review the performance of teams and individuals.

Sales Cycle- The length of time it takes to close a deal from your first touch to the close.

Buying Window- The time when a prospect/company is evaluating different products/solutions to implement.